First published in Great Britain by
Pendulum Gallery Press
56 Ackender Road, Alton, Hants GU34 1JS

© TONI GOFFE 1986

IS THERE SEX AFTER 40?
ISBN 0-948912-02-2

REPRINTED 1987, 1988, 1989, 1990, 1991

PRINTED IN GREAT BRITAIN BY
UNWIN BROTHERS LTD, OLD WOKING, SURREY

-" I REMEMBER WHEN, THE ONLY THING YOU WANTED TO TAKE TO BED, WAS **ME** ! "-

" CARRY ON DAD, WE'RE JUST HAVING A SEX EDUCATION
CLASS FOR OUR TOYS......."

" OH NO! THEY'RE AT IT AGAIN! "

" MUMMY, THIS IS SARAH WHO WILL BE SHARING MY ROOM AND OUR LIVES TOGETHER FROM NOW ON......"-

" IT USED TO BE 'NOT TILL THE KIDS ARE ASLEEP', NOW IT'S 'HURRY, BEFORE THEY GET BACK FROM THE PUB'!" -

"MY MEANINGFUL RELATIONSHIP WITH RODNEY IS NOW
VACUUM·ORIENTATED!"-

"- YOU KNOW WHAT I MISS ZELDA, THE CHILDRENS LAUGHTER!" -

"YES, I KNOW WE'RE SEPARATED, BUT HE KEEPS COMING BACK TO APOLOGISE !!" -

"GEORGE, BE GENTLE WITH ME ...."

" NOT NOW, RUFUS, ... NOT **<u>NOW!</u>** " -

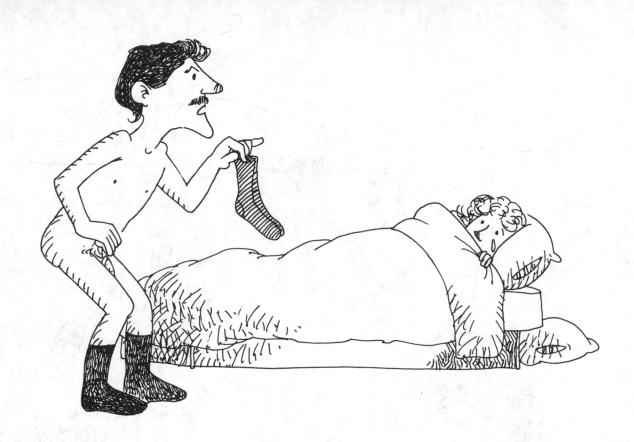

"LET'S TRY IT AGAIN, WITH SOCKS ON........"-

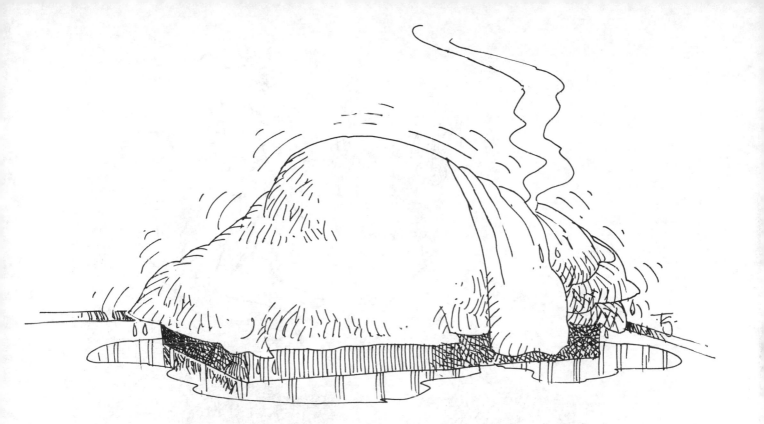

" JOHN, I THINK THE ELECTRIC BLANKET IS STILL
SWITCHED ON...."-

'MORE! ANGELA, **MORE**!...'

-" IT'S ALRIGHT, HE'S JUST WORRIED ABOUT ME...."-

-" HAVE YOU EVER THOUGHT OF GETTING YOUR EYES TESTED....."-

-" GEORGE, HAS JUST FINISHED THE KARMA SUTRA AND THE
KARMA SUTRA HAS JUST ABOUT FINISHED GEORGE!"-

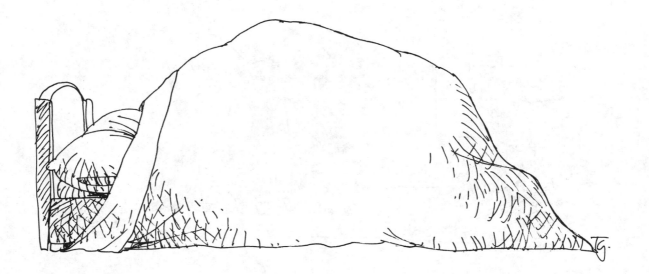

- "OH DAMN! THE BATTERY'S RUN OUT!" -

" ARTHUR, THE DOG'S LAUGHING AGAIN....'"-

"WELL IF HE'S NOT YOUR FRIEND, WHO'S FRIEND IS HE?"—

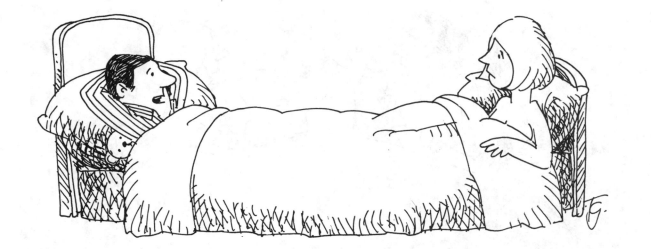

"WELL, IS OUR TRIAL SEPARATION WORKING OUT OR ISN'T IT?"

–" I SUPPOSE THIS IS JUST ANOTHER SORDID LITTLE AFFAIR TO YOU, GEORGE "–

_" WELL, YOU TRY FITTING AN AFFAIR IN BETWEEN
SHOPPING AND THE VETS....."-

-" WAIT GEORGE, I HAVE THIS STRANGE FEELING WE'RE BEING WATCHED! "-

-" IT'S NOT WHAT YOU THINK, HILDA!"-

" AFTERTHOUGHT? NO, AFTER SEX ACTUALLY " -

-"WELL, <u>I</u> USUALLY SLEEP ON THAT SIDE IN <u>MY</u> HOME!"-

-"THAT'S A COINCIDENCE, NEITHER DOES MY WIFE'S EXHUSBAND'S LOVER'S GIRLFRIEND...."-

" – MY WIFE'S JUST LEFT ME !... " –

-"THE COMPUTER SAYS 'TONIGHT'S THE NIGHT." "-

"NOW, WHAT WAS IT I HAD TO REMEMBER TONIGHT?" -

–" I'M SORRY DEAR, I JUST DON'T FEEL LIKE IT TONIGHT....."–

-" ..... AND TO GEORGE, I LEAVE MY MISTRESS, GLORIA, AND
THE BONDAGE EQUIPMENT ...... "-

" I'M NOT SURE I WANT TO BRING ANIMALS INTO MY SEX LIFE, JUST AT THIS MOMENT, ARTHUR......."-

—" YOU DON'T NEED YOUR GLASSES, WE HAVE A BRAILLE
SITUATION HERE "—

"WELL, IF IT HURTS YOUR BACK, YOU SHOULDN'T DO IT!".

" A FINE FIGURE OF <u>TWO</u> MEN, I'D SAY....."-

" HELLO THERE, LONG TIME NO SEE ......" -

"WELL, I SEE SOMETHING UNDER THERE, IN THE SHADOWS" –

"THERE MUST BE <u>ONE</u>, WE COULD TRY?"

"GEORGE, IT SAYS HERE, THAT NORMAL COUPLES
DO IT, **AT LEAST ONCE AWEEK!**"–

" ARE YOU GOING TO SLEEP, OR DO YOU WANT TO
FOOL-AROUND ?"-

"DO YOU REMEMBER BED, BEFORE TELEVISION?"

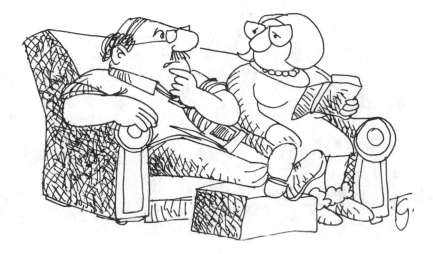

-"I STILL GET THE URGE, BUT I CAN'T REMEMBER WHAT FOR ....." -

-"WOW! WHAT A GREAT PROGRAMME, NOW, WHAT
WERE WE DOING?"-

-" YOUR 'GO-FOR-IT' HAS 'GONE-FOR-IT'! "-

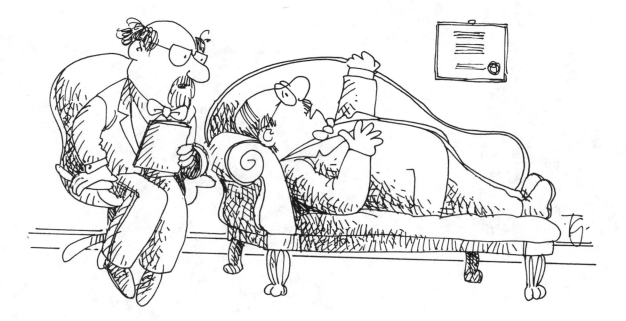

–"I'M GETTING TOO OLD FOR A MID-LIFE CRISIS"–

- " I LIKED YOU BETTER, WHEN THAT BULGE
WAS IN YOUR TROUSERS "-

-" WELL, I'D LIKE TO RE-LIVE <u>MY</u> YOUTH IN A WARM HOTEL ROOM "-

"YOU REMEMBER ME WILLIAM, I USED TO 'GET YOU' IN THE BIKE SHED AT SCHOOL!"-

"WE MET AT A WINE AND CHEESE CAKE PARTY" -

"AH, DOES RESTING UP ON A SATURDAY AFTERNOON, MEAN YOU'LL BE FRESH AND READY TO SEDUCE ME TONIGHT?" –

-" GROUP SEX, IS SOMETHING I'VE ALWAYS WANTED TO GET INTO"-

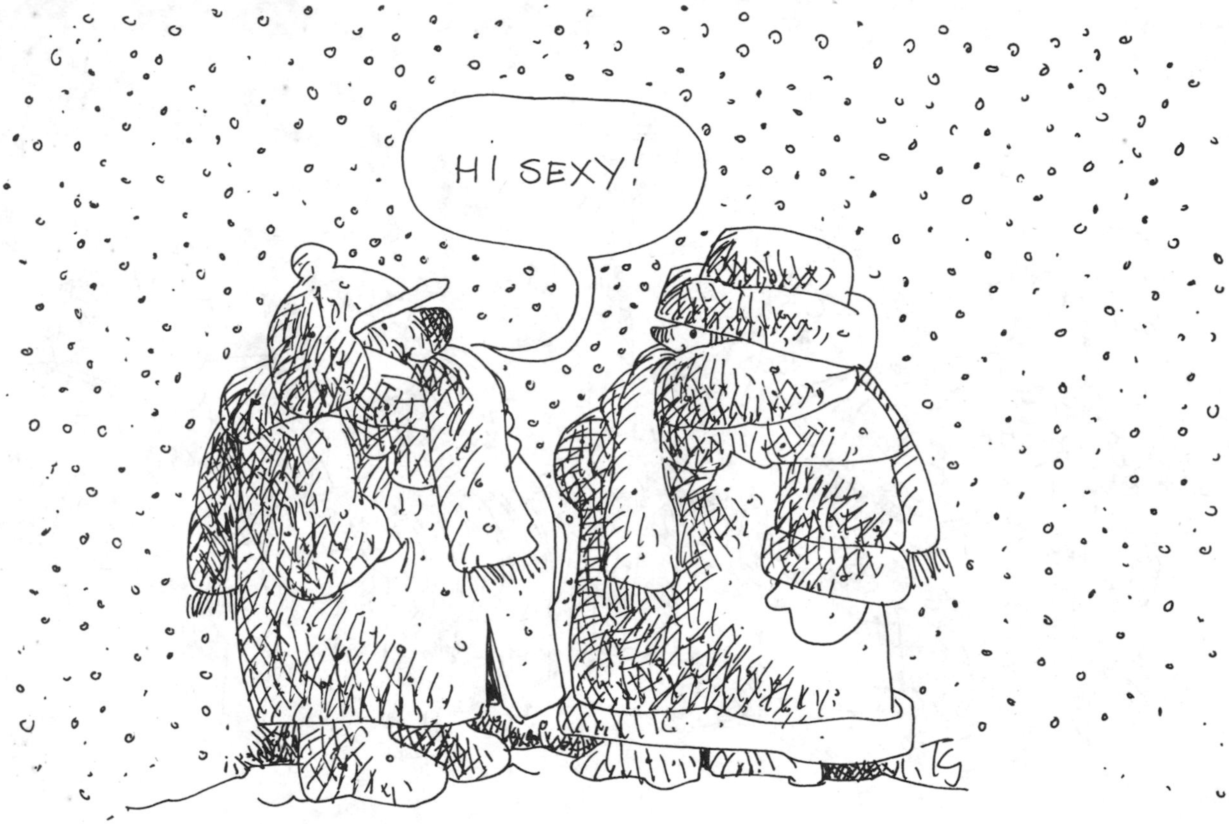
HI SEXY!
TG